FACTORS IMPROVE SOCIAL DEVELOPMENT

JOHN LOK

First Printing: Jan 2021

Contents

Preface

Introduction

Nowadays, human must hope have comfortable lives. Every one must need comfortable feeling to live in our earth in any country. I write this book aims to give my opinion whether what aspects are our most hope in order we can live more comfortable as well as owning safe feeling. I shall concentrate on researching these several aspects that I feel we need to concern how to improve if we hope that we can live more comfortable and satisfactory and safe in our future lives.

These several aspects that I research my include: How and why can reduce global environmental pollution to bring our advantages ? How and why can improve internet technology development to bring our advantage? How and why can improve medicine health discovery to bring our advantage? How and why can improve living environment to bring our advantage? How and why can improve social welfare to bring our advantage ?

Readers can have more clear understanding to analyze whether above these different social aspects that they will be our future main solution or improvement in order to let we can live more comfortable and safe and satisfactory in our earth.

Prologue

Table of content

CHAPTER ONE

REDUCING GLOBAL ENVIRONMENTAL POLLUTION ADVANTAGES

What are the advantages to reduce global environmental pollution to our future societies? If we do not continue to avoid to cause air and water pollution from manufacture or driving car etc. business or enjoyment activities, what negative influences what are caused to our future societies? I shall attempt to explain as below:

Firstly , I shall discuss whether reducing greenhouse gases benefits air quality how and why it can save human future lives. Air quality "co-benefits" result mainly from reductions in air pollutant emissions from the same sources that emit greenhouse gases. For example, replacing a coal-fired power plant with a renewable electricity source, such as wind power, reduces both air pollutant and greenhouse gas emissions. Nowadays, our world has been slow to adopt significant actions to address climate change, as it is a long-term and global problem. The benefits of reducing carbon dioxide today are felt in the future, and since they occur globally, countries may take little action and rely on others to lead. On the other hand, better air quality and improved health are realized rapidly and locally, providing government leaders with tangible benefits from their actions to reduce carbon dioxide. For example, reducing greenhouse gases pollution , it can bring health benefits of Air Pollution Reduction to influence global has more fresh air to let we can breathe, then we can avoid air pollution breath to cause our lung hurt, even death easily. Air pollution is a grave risk to human health that affects nearly everyone in the world and nearly every organ in the body. Fortunately, it is largely a preventable risk. Reducing pollution at its source can have a rapid and substantial impact on health. Within a few weeks, respiratory and irritation symptoms, such as shortness of breath, cough, phlegm, and sore throat, disappear; school absenteeism, clinic visits, hospitalizations, premature births, cardiovascular illness and death, and all-cause mortality decrease significantly. The interventions are cost-effective. Reducing factors causing air pollution and climate change have strong cobenefits. Although regions with high air pollution have the greatest potential for health benefits, health improvements continue to be associated with pollution decreases even below international standards. The large response to and short time needed for benefits of these interventions emphasize the urgency of improving global air quality and the importance of increasing efforts to reduce pollution at local levels.

● The consequences of water and air and water and chemical pollution

Air pollution may bring these effects. Diseases such as amoebiasis, typhoid and hookworm are caused by polluted drinking water.Water polluted by chemicals such as heavy metals, lead, pesticides and hydrocarbon can cause hormonal and reproductive.A polluted beach causes rashes, hepatitis, gastroenteritis, diarrhea, encephalitis, stomach aches and vomiting. Pollution or the introduction of different forms of waste materials in our environment has negative effects to the ecosystem we rely on. How does pollution affect the ecosystem? There are many kinds of pollution, but the ones that have the most impact to us are Air and Water pollution.Pollution or the introduction of different forms of waste materials in our environment has negative effects to the ecosystem we rely on. There are many kinds of pollution, but the ones that have the most impact to us are Air and Water pollution. How does pollution affect humans? Harmful gases and particles in the air come from a range of sources, including exhaust fumes from vehicles, smoke from burning coal or gas, and tobacco smoke. There are ways to limit the effects of air pollution on health, such as avoiding areas with heavy traffic. Thus, air pollutants cause less-direct health effects when they contribute to climate change. Heat waves, extreme weather, food supply disruptions, and other effects related to increased greenhouse gases can have negative impacts on human health.

There are many kinds of pollution, but the ones that have the most impact to us are Air, Water, and chemical pollution. How does pollution affect humans? In the following paragraphs, we will enumerate the consequences of releasing pollutants in the environment. We cause most of the pollution and we will suffer the consequences if we don't stop. We are already seeing its effects in the form of global warming, contaminated seafood, increased cases of lung diseases and more.

We release a variety of chemicals into the atmosphere when we burn the fossil fuels we use every day. We breathe air to live and what we breathe has a direct impact on our health. Over 100 million years of healthy life are lost every single year as a result of air pollution. On average, that's the same as 1 year and 8 months of healthy life lost for every single person on Earth.

Air pollution is the world's 4th most lethal killer

Air pollution is the cause of 8.9 million deaths globally every year. That means that every 4 seconds, someone somewhere on the planet dies from air pollution. The UN has called air pollution the world's worst environmental health risk. Air pollution is also the world's 4th most lethal killer (following malnutrition, unsafe sex, and the lack of safe, clean water and sanitation).

Air pollution from car exhaust affects human reproduction

If pregnant women are exposed to air pollution from car exhaust, it can alter the structure of the chromosomes in the fetus and increase the risks of cancer and various birth defects.

Air pollution and climate change closely linked

The main cause of air pollution as well as climate change (CO2-emissions) is the burning of fossil fuels (oil, coal, gas). A change to greener alternatives such as solar or wind power will therefore help both the climate and human health.

How air pollution influences human health

Breathing polluted air puts you at a higher risk for asthma and other respiratory diseases. When exposed to ground ozone for 6 to 7 hours, scientific evidence show that healthy people's lung function decreased and they suffered from respiratory inflammation.Air pollutants are mostly carcinogens and living in a polluted area can put people at risk of Cancer.

Coughing and wheezing are common symptoms observed on city folks.

Damages the immune system, endocrine and reproductive systems. High levels of particle pollution have been associated with higher incidents of heart problems.The burning of fossil fuels and the release of carbon dioxide in the atmosphere are causing the Earth to become warmer. Read about the effects of Global Warming here.The toxic chemicals released into the air settle into plants and water sources. Animals eat the contaminated plants and drink the water. The poison then travels up the food chain – to us.

Water Pollution Effects

Just like the air we breathe, water is vital to our survival. We need clean water to drink, to irrigate our crops and the fish we eat live in the waters. We play in rivers, lakes and streams – we live near bodies of water. It's a precious resource that can easily be polluted and the contamination can be transferred to us and affect our health.

The consumer society is powered by water

Everything we buy, use, eat takes water to produce. Our total use of water through the stuff we buy is represented by "The water footprint". The global water footprint is 9 trillion tons per year or almost 300,000 tons per second.

The consumer society is getting more and more thirsty

Global demand for freshwater is projected to increase 55 % between 2000 and 2050. By 2050, it will reach a massive 5500 square kilometers or 5.5 trillion tons. The main sources for the rise in freshwater use are industry and manufacturing with an expected increase of 400 %. In addition, water demand from electricity-generation will increase 140 % and domestic use 130 %.

The pollution of groundwater resources is increasing

280 billion tons of groundwater is being polluted annually. In 2000, Earth's groundwater resources were being polluted twice as fast as in 1960. Water polluted by chemicals such as heavy metals, lead, pesticides and hydrocarbon can cause hormonal and reproductive problems, damage to the nervous system, liver and kidney damage and cancer – to name a few. Being exposed to mercury causes Parkinson's disease, Alzheimer's, heart disease and death. A polluted beach causes rashes, hepatitis, gastroenteritis, diarrhea, encephalitis, stomach aches and vomiting.Water pollution affects marine life which is one of our food sources. Remember the stories of contaminated shellfish and how those who ate them died?

Plastic pollution

Plastic wasn't invented until the late 1800s and the production of plastic didn't take off until around 1950. But then it really took off. The world has produced over 9 billion tons of plastic since around 1950. 6.3 billion tons (over two thirds!) of this plastic have ended up in the environment - including our oceans. By 2025, there will be a staggering 100 bags of plastic for each foot of coastline in the world! At this point, the ocean will contain around one ton of plastic for every three tons of fish. By 2050, there could be more plastic than fish (by weight) in the world's oceans. Just imagine. Diseases such as amoebiasis, typhoid and hookworm are caused by polluted drinking water.

We live in an ecosystem where the action of one has the potential to affect the many. This can be a good or a bad thing, depending on what the action is. Our mistakes has polluted the environment that we live in and we are waking up and owning to the fact. We are trying to reverse the damage. The good news is that every positive action counts. The small effort you make towards a greener environment can start a healing ripple effect. We may still save what is left of our natural resources and make the world a better place to live in for our future generation.

Chemical pollution

Global production of synthetic chemicals is around 250 billion tons a year. Many of these chemicals find their way into our bodies and the consequences are horrifying. In samples from human beings, a study found as many as 420 different chemicals known to or suspected of causing cancer.Another study found an average of 200 industrial chemicals present in the cord blood of newborn babies.

287 different chemicals were identified in the cord blood.

180 can cause cancer

217 are toxic to the brain and nervous system

208 can cause birth defects or abnormal development.

This is truly terrifying. Especially since the global production of synthetic chemicals is expected to increase six-fold between 2000 and 2050.

On average, we already have around 700 synthetic chemicals in our body that are not a natural part of the human body chemistry. And we know very little about how the combination of these chemicals will affect us.

● Reducing air and water and plastic and chemical pollution different policies implement will be needed to different countries in our future societies.

Over the last decades, energy and pollution control policies combined with structural changes in the economy decoupled emission trends from economic growth, increasingly also in the developing world. It is found that effective implementation of the presently decided national pollution control regulations should allow further economic growth without major deterioration of ambient air quality, but will not be enough to reduce pollution levels in many world regions. A combination of ambitious policies focusing on pollution controls, energy and climate, agricultural production systems and addressing human consumption habits could drastically improve air quality throughout the world. By 2040, mean population exposure to PM2.5 from anthropogenic sources could be reduced by about 75% relative to 2015 and brought well below the WHO guideline in large areas of the world. While the implementation of the proposed technical measures is likely to be technically feasible in the future, the transformative changes of current practices will require strong political will, supported by a full appreciation of the multiple benefits. Improved air quality would avoid a large share of the current 3–9 million cases of premature deaths annually. At the same time, the measures that deliver clean air would also significantly reduce emissions of greenhouse gases and contribute to multiple UN sustainable development goals.

Given the dynamics of these factors and their complex interplay, what could be expected for future air quality around the world, and which determinants will be dominating? To answer this question, this paper identifies key factors that contributed to historic air pollution trends in different world regions, outlines conceivable ranges of their future development and examines their interplay on global air quality in the next decades. In particular, the paper provides a fresh perspective on how ambitious policy interventions could achieve clean air worldwide.

● Future projections of air pollutant emissions

A range of studies in the scientific literature explored the implications of these findings on future emissions and air quality. For a long time, future global air pollutant trends were mainly modelled in the context of long-term greenhouse gas emission scenarios . The early global studies on air pollutant emissions, notably the scenarios developed for the 'Special Report on

Emissions Scenarios' and the 'Representative Concentration Pathways' that have been prepared for the Intergovernmental Panel on Climate Change (IPCC) proposed declining trends of (energy-related) air pollutants, due to autonomous technological progress and assumed pollution control policies along the environmental Kuznets hypothesis. Later, the improved understanding of the importance of targeted air quality policy interventions motivated a more differentiated approach to projections of air pollutant emissions, resulting in a wider range of air pollutant trajectories than in previous global scenarios. At the same time, the climate community addressed the interactions between decarbonization strategies and air pollutant emissions, both with the interest to reveal health benefits from low carbon policies and to explore the combined impacts of long-lived greenhouse gases and short-lived air pollutants (e.g. SO2 and black carbon) on radiative forcing and temperature increase . In general, the literature reveals strong impacts of ambitious decarbonization strategies on energy-related air pollutants SO2, NOx and PM, due to the phase-out of fossil fuels and the containment of all flue gases connected with carbon capture and storage. However, enhanced use of biomass as a greenhouse gas policy measure may lead to higher PM emissions . Compared to the climate-focused analyses that deal mainly with energy-related emissions and the role of climate policy interventions, only a few studies addressed the longer-term prospects for air pollution from a health- and ecosystems perspective. These studies take full account of other sources that also contribute substantially to population exposure to harmful air pollution, such as agricultural activities, waste management and materials handling. Also, they developed a more holistic approach towards the understanding of future trends in nitrogen emissions and their health and environmental impacts.

● How air pollution may influence the course of pandemics

The COVID-19 pandemic is causing devastating mortality, with the highest rates of intensive care unit hospitalization and morbidity among older adults, men, and those with certain preexisting conditions, most notably cardiopulmonary diseases, obesity, and diabetes. In addition, a host of interrelated socioeconomic factors—including race, ethnicity, occupation, and poverty—increase the risks of COVID-19 infection for people of color, health care professionals, and other essential workers. These factors are, in turn, influenced by conditions of the human environment including chronic levels of air pollution, most notably fine particulate matter (PM2.5) that is a well-established risk factor for death from cardiovascular and pulmonary obstructive diseases. This raises the question of whether long-term exposure to higher levels of PM2.5 increases the severity of COVID-19 and, if so, what measures might be taken to ameliorate those risks. This is the challenge addressed by Wu et al. in a new contribution to a developing series of papers for Science Advances that is dedicated to the study of pandemics from an environmental perspective.The ideal way to address questions about how PM2.5 pollution might influence the course of the pandemic would involve the study of detailed health datasets for very large numbers of people from all walks of life and locations. In this way, the potential effects of PM2.5 pollution might be evaluated in the context of other details about each individual's life history and conditions. The amount of time required for rigorous, extensive studies, however, conflicts with the swift nature of the COVID-19 pandemic. Addressing the potential impact of air pollution on COVID-19 mortality requires a more nimble approach to environmental policy decision-making.

COVID-19–related death counts (compiled by Johns Hopkins University for more than 3000 U.S. counties) and well-established PM2.5 pollution levels for each county. The results show that higher values of exposure to PM2.5 are positively correlated with higher county-level mortality after taking into account over 20 potentially confounding factors. Most notably, they conclude that an increase of just 1 μg/m3 in the long-term average of pollution is associated with a significant 11% increase in a county's rate of mortality.There are strong policy implications for these results. COVID-19, zoonotic influenza, and other potentially severe emerging zoonotic diseases are and will remain long-term threats to our species. Rapidly emerging datasets suggest that these threats are likely to be exacerbated by air pollution, even at the levels currently attained in the United States despite conscientious efforts to improve air quality. While incomplete and not yet fully vetted by the broader scientific community, pathfinding studies such as that of Wu et al. set the stage for more traditional environmental epidemiology research.

● Benefits of Reducing and Reusing policy

Recucing and reusing policy may help our earth to avoid serious pollution influences , such as prevents pollution caused by reducing the need to harvest new raw materials, saves energy, reduces greenhouse gas emissions that contribute to global climate change, helps sustain the environment for future generations, reduces the amount of waste that will need to be recycled or sent to landfills and incinerators and allows products to be used to their fullest extent.

● Ideas on How to Reduce and Reuse to implement

Buy used. You can find everything from clothes to building materials at specialized reuse centers and consignment shops. Often, used items are less expensive and just as good as new. Look for products that use less packaging. When manufacturers make their products with less packaging, they use less raw material. This reduces waste and costs. These extra savings can be passed along to the consumer. Buying in bulk, for example, can reduce packaging and save money. Buy reusable over disposable items. Look for items that can be reused; the little things can add up. For example, you can bring your own silverware and cup to work, rather than using disposable items. Maintain and repair products, like clothing, tires and appliances, so that they won't have to be thrown out and replaced as frequently. Borrow, rent or share items that are used infrequently, like party decorations, tools or furniture.

Thus, we are living in our earth. We are everyone has responsibilities to do environmental protection activities in every day, such as reduce and reuse activity will be our right environmental protection daily behavior, walking replaces to reducing to driving when we need short time to arrive the destination in any time, manufacturers need to buy air and water clean machines to avoid serious air and water pollution in their factory manufacturing processes, we need to reduce the frequeny to travel, e.g. one to two times travelling by air planes every year, then sky will have much fresh air in our earth, also airlines need to shorten flying time , e.g. New Zealand airlines only fly to Australia near distance country , it can not fly to US, or UK far away distance countries, China airlines only fly to Singapore, Japan etc. near distance Asia countries, they do not fly to US, UK far away disrance countries. Then, our future environment pollution will be reduced as well as we can have much fresh air to breathe and drive clean water to proplong our lives when we have health.

CHAPTER TWO

IMPROVING INTERNET TECHNOLOGY DEVELOPMENT

Why do we improve to improve internet technology? What long term social benefits will benefits if scientists can improve internet speed and reseach any information function ? I shall research these questions to give suggestion as below:

Why does internet improvement make life better? Internet of Things Benefits In short, the scale of change that IoT technology offers can be scary. At the same time, the benefits of a well-executed IoT strategy can be more need for an organization: Safety, Comfort, Efficiency. Also, the Internet offers teens the ability to make friends with peers with whom they would not otherwise connect. With pop culture deteriorating into many distinct subcultures, teens' interests are more variable than they have ever been.With internet communication, employees can effortlessly communicate with one another at anytime from anywhere in the world. This allows employees situated in different parts of the world to give their opinion and voice their concerns. Through internet access, individuals in developing countries are able to gain access to more of the modern economy. With internet connectivity, those living in remote areas can now easily take out microloans, participate in e-banking and more. A large share of respondents predict enormous potential for improved quality of life over the next 50 years for most individuals thanks to internet connectivity, although many said the benefits of a wired world are not likely to be evenly distributed.

● How internet can excite young to learn?

Internet can learn youngs to learn much different new knowlege when they research any questions and find answers from internet channel.

As one major aspect of teen life is social environment, changes in how teens connect impact the ways in which teens develop social skills. ** Luckily, the Internet offers many social-skill enhancement opportunities for teens of all different personalities . One advantage the Internet brings that the standard school environment cannot is the ability for teens to adjust their amount of social interaction. Teens who are extremely outgoing can spend their free time in social environments both offline and online, making new connections and catching up with friends.For example, a teen who finds large amounts of face-to-face interaction to be intimidating can use the Internet to engage in conversations while reducing the potential for social anxiety. In a way, this trains less social teens to be more social . In the past, these types of teens did not have the advantage of this social training provided by the Internet.

● Internet can encourage Social Network Growth

The Internet offers teens the ability to make friends with peers with whom they would not otherwise connect. With pop culture deteriorating into many distinct subcultures, teens' interests are more variable than they have ever been. Whereas in the past, children at school might have discussed the current top 40 when discussing music, today's kids define their musical tastes as specific genres, such as post-industrial, dubstep or jpop. Today, it's harder for teens to find peers who share the same interests in their schools.

But online, not so. The Internet's social networks help teens find communities of peers who share similar interests, allowing a teen to grow his social network in a way that is specific to him 2. Today's teens are increasingly willing to make friends with different groups of people due to the ability to actually meet them, and this can be useful when they reach adulthood, a time in which accepting people of different backgrounds and demographics is crucial to career and academic growth. The Internet offers teens the ability to make friends with peers with whom they would not otherwise connect.

Today's teens are increasingly willing to make friends with different groups of people due to the ability to actually meet them, and this can be useful when they reach adulthood, a time in which accepting people of different backgrounds and demographics is crucial to career and academic growth.But the Internet can help teens foster self identity through exposure to new people, communities, hobbies and concepts. As teens go through more experiences, they learn more about themselves. And as the Internet can offer teens a wealth of experience, it can play the role of hastening the development of self identity.For many teens, the hardest part of life is figuring out identity.But the Internet can help teens foster self identity through exposure to new people, communities, hobbies and concepts.

● What Are Main Benefits of Internet Communication speed improvement ?

It may include as below:

1 Makes communication easier

Doing business through phone or mail doesn't work well ? Before the internet came into existence, the only way to communicate was through a phone. Or if you needed to send a note you had to send letters via mail. With the arrival of the Internet, staff and team managers can connect instantaneously without leaving their work place. ezTalks Meetings, a one-stop internet communication provider, is a perfect example. With this platform, participants can communicate as if they were right next to one another thanks to its quality video and audio. The tool comes with a rich set of features like screen sharing, cross platform chat, innovative whiteboard, and more.

2 Enhances collaboration

Internet communication brings teams together across the globe. Staff can collaborate easily without limitations and make more informed decisions instantaneously. This leads to reduced project timelines, cutting back on the time required to launch a new product/service. This piece of technology is also useful in education. Not only can students collaborate with foreign students, they can share ideas and learn about the diverse cultures out there. Parents can also become actively involved in their kids education by linking their children school with libraries, homes, and more. Millions of schools around the world are already using this technology to enhance learning.

3 It is cost effective

The cost of internet communication is significantly low when compared with other means of communication like face to face meetings and mail delivery. The technology connects you to your partners, colleagues, clients and suppliers from just about any location for a fraction of the cost required to host a one-on-one meeting. And as technology continues to become more efficient, the cost of online communication continues to drop significantly. With the traditional face to face meeting, you need to spare time, cash to travel and so on. Internet communication allows you and your team to connect without having to leave your offices.

4 Improves work relationships

Building a good relationship between workers spread around the globe is not easy. Business trips can negatively affect life– work balance. Team members can burn out fast if they have to make business travels that deny them the chance to participate in crucial events with friends and family. With internet communication, employees can effortlessly communicate with one another at anytime from anywhere in the world. This allows employees situated in different parts of the world to give their opinion and voice their concerns. Therefore, internet communication is an important business asset, particularly for companies that have tapped into global markets.

5 Increases productivity

While the companies of yesteryear might not have treasured effective communication, modern workplace requires both the management and the staff have the tools to effectively communicate internally and externally. This is because effective communication is important in increasing productivity as it directly impacts the behavior of the employees and how they perform. Internet communication plays an integral role in getting stuff done fast and efficiently which ultimately improves productivity. Poor communication can have a negative effect on productivity as the staff may not get the adequate info to accomplish a job they have been assigned.

6 Increases accountability

Errors slow down productivity and so it is tempting to punish or fire employees who repeatedly make errors. One major advantage of internet communication is that it helps to decrease these errors. This piece of technology pinpoints errors and how staff can avoid them. In workplaces that don't make use of various forms of internet communication, those mistakes go unnoticed. With internet communication, there is no room for mistakes as employees feel liable for their actions and safe to point out mistakes. They also feel secure expressing their ideas and suggestions in a group setting.

- Why does internet improvement can help any industries services or efficiencies improvment?

Internet improvement will revolutionize the world and lead to groundbreaking changes in transportation, industry, communication, education, energy, health care, communication, entertainment, government, warfare and even basic research. For example, self-driving cars, trains, semi-trucks, ships and airplanes will mean that goods and people can be transported farther, faster and with less energy and with massively fewer vehicles. Automated mining and manufacturing will further reduce the need for human workers to engage in rote work. Machine language translation will finally close the language barrier, while digital tutors, teachers and personal assistants with human qualities will make everything from learning new subjects to booking salon appointments faster and easier. For businesses, automated secretaries, salespeople, waiters, waitress, baristas and customer support personnel will lead to cost savings, efficiency gains and improved customer experiences. Socially, individuals will be able to find AI pets, friends and even therapists who can provide the love and emotional support that many people so desperately want. Entertainment will become far more interactive, as immersive AI experiences come to supplement traditional passive forms of media. Energy generation and health care will vastly improve with the addition of powerful AI tools that can take a systems-level view of operations and locate opportunities to gain efficiencies in design and operation. AI-driven robotics (e.g., drones) will revolutionize warfare. Finally, intelligent AI will contribute immensely to basic research and likely begin to create scientific discoveries of its own. So, it implies that internet improvement ought assist any kinds of industy service or efficiency improvement.

● Internet may become any organizational digital assets

On an individual basis, we will think about our digital assets as much as our physical ones. Ideally, we will have more transparent control over our data, and the ability to understand where it resides and exchange it for value – negotiating with the platform companies that are now in a winner-take-all position. Some children born today are named with search engine-optimization in mind; we'll be thinking more comprehensively about a set of rights and responsibilities of personal data that children are born with. Governments will have a higher level of regulation and protection of individual data. On an individual level, there will be greater integration of technology with our physical selves. For example, I can see devices that augment hearing and vision, and that enable greater access to data through our physical selves. Hard for me to picture what that looks like, but 50 years is a lot of time to figure it out. On a societal level, AI will have affected many jobs. Not only the truck drivers and the factory workers, but professions that have been largely unassailable – law, medicine – will have gone through a painful transformation. It seems entirely reasonable that a great deal of our digital lives will be focused on habitable environments: identifying them, improving them, expanding them.

Significant, often highly communication and computation technologically driven, advances in day-to-day areas like health care, safety and human services, will continue to have a significant measurable improvement in many lives, often 'invisible' as an unnoticed reduction in bad outcomes, will continue to reduce the incidence of human-scale disasters. Advances in opportunities for self-actualisation through education, community and creative work will continue. So, I believe that future many organizations may apply internet communication tool for their digital assets.

- Internet improvement may assist robotic development

Most of the focus on technology and particularly AI and machine learning developments these days is limited to virtual systems (e.g., apps for travel booking, social networks, search engines, games). I expect this to move, in the next 50 years, into networking people with machines, remotely operating in a myriad of environments, such as homes, hospitals, factories, sport arenas and so on. This will change work as we know it today, as it will change medicine (increasing remote surgery), travel (autonomous and remotely-guided cars, trains, planes), entertainment (games where real robots, instead of virtual agents, evolve in real scenarios). These are just a few ideas/scenarios. Many more, difficult to anticipate today, will appear. They will bring further challenges on privacy, security and safety, which everyone should be closely watching and monitoring. Beyond current discussions on privacy problems concerning 'virtual world' apps, we need to consider that 'real world' apps may enhance many of those problems, as they interact physically and/or in proximity with humans. So, future historians will observe that, in many ways, the rise of the internet over the next few decades will have improved the world, but it hasn't been without its costs that were sometimes severe and disruptive to entire industries and nations as well as improve robotic development.

This is similarly valid for AI.Living longer and better lives is the shining promise of the digital age. Many respondents to this canvassing agreed that internet advancement is likely to lead to better human-health outcomes, although perhaps not for everyone. As the following comments show, experts foresee new cures for chronic illnesses, rapid advancement in biotechnology and expanded access to care thanks to the development of better telehealth systems. Life will improve in multiple ways. One in particular I think worth mentioning will be improvements in health care in three distinct ways. One is significantly better medical technology related to cancer and other major diseases. The second is significantly reduced cost of health care. The third is much higher and broader availability of high-quality health care, thereby reducing the differences in outcomes between wealthy and poor citizens. So, when hospitals can improve internet communication , if the hospital can apply robots to assist doctors and nurses to serve patients. Then, internet communication can help them to cooperate more efficient.

- Internet improvement to assist 5G laptop development

Many of the technologies we see commercialized today began in government and university research labs. Fifty years ago, computers were the size of walk-in closets, and the notion of personal computers was laughable to most people. Today we're facing another shift, from personal and mobile to ambient computing. We're also seeing a huge amount of research in the areas of prosthetics, neuroscience and other technologies intended to translate brain activity into physical form. All discussion of transhumanism aside, there are very real current and future applications for technology 'implants' and prosthetics that will be able to aid mobility, memory, even intelligence, and other physical and neurological functions. And, as nearly always happens, the technology is far ahead of our understanding of the human implications. Will these technologies be available to all, or just to a privileged class? What happens to the data? Will it be 'willed' as a digital legacy to future generations? What are the ethical (and for some, religious and spiritual) implications of changing the human body with technology? In many ways, these are not new questions. We've used technology to augment the physical form since the first caveman picked up a walking stick. But the key here will be to focus as much (or more) on the way we use these technologies as we do on inventing them. All of above factors will be influenced to future 5G mobile phone by internet improvement?

Our homes, transportation, appliances, communication devices and even our clothes will be constantly communicating as part of a digital network. We have enough pieces of this today that we can somewhat imagine what it will be like. Through our clothes, doctors can monitor in real time our vital signs, metabolic condition and markers relevant to specific diseases. Parents will have real-time information about young children. The difference in the future will be the constant sharing of information, data updates and responses of all these interconnected devices. The things we create will interact with us to protect us. Our notions of privacy and even liability will be redefined. Lowering the cost and increasing the effectiveness of health care will require sharing information about how our bodies are functioning. Those who opt out may have to accept palliative hospice care over active treatment. Not keeping track of children real-time may be considered a form of child neglect. Digital will do more than connect our things to each other – it will invade our bodies. Advances in prosthetics, replacement organs and implants will turn our bodies into digital devices. This will create a host of new issues, including defining 'human' and where the line exists between that human and the digital universe – if people are always connected, always on are humans now part of the internet?

● How internet improvement influences AI provides medical service to hospitals?

Similarly, AI embedded in devices or wearables can be applied to predict and ameliorate many mental health illnesses. However, there is potential for there to be huge inequalities in our societies in the ability of individuals to access such technologies, causing both social disruption and new causes for mental health diseases, such as depression and anxiety. On balance, I am an optimist about the ability of human beings to adjust and develop new ethical norms for dealing with such issues.Surveillance technology, especially that powered by AI algorithms, is becoming more powerful and all-present than ever before. But to look at that and say that technology won't help people is absurd. Medical technology, technology to help people with disabilities, technology that will increase our comfort and abilities as humans will continue to appear and develop.The digital revolution will bring benefits in particular for health, providing personalized monitoring through Internet of Things and wearable devices. The AI will analyze those data in order to provide personalized medicine solutions.The most noticeable change for better in the next 50 years will be in health and average life expectancy. At this pace, and, taking into account the developments in digital technologies, I hope that several discoveries will reduce the risk of death, such as cancer or even death by road accident. New drugs could be developed, increasing the active work age and possibility maintaining the sustainability of countries' social health care and retirement funds. Another area AI can have impact is in creating the framework within genomics, epigenomics and metabolomics can be used to keep people healthy and to intervene when we start to deviate from health. Indeed, with AI we may be able to hack the brain and other secreting cells so that we can auto-generate lifesaving medicines, block unwanted biological processes (e.g., cancer), and coupled to understanding the brain, be able to hack at neurological disorders."

Thus, I believe that future hospitals were able to utilize internet technology to solve human health problems to make citizens' lives better and improve their access to care and services to improve their health outcomes. The benefits of the internet in the health care industry have continued to improve access to care and services, particularly for elderly, disabled or rural citizens. Digital tools will continue to be integrated into daily life to help the most vulnerable and isolated who need services, care and support. With laws supporting these groups, benefits in these areas will continue and expand to include behavioral health and resources for this group and for others. In the area of behavioral health in particular, digital tools will provide far-reaching benefits to citizens who need services but do not access them directly in person. Access to behavioral health will increase significantly in the next 50 years as a result of more enhanced and widely available digital tools made available to practitioners for delivering care to vulnerable populations, and by minimizing the stigma of accessing this type of care in person. It is a more affordable, personalized and continuous way of providing this type of care that is also more likely to attain adherence.

● The cyborg generation: Humans will partner more directly with technology when internet is popular to be used in any where

The inevitable 'Singularity' will result in changes to humans and will increase the rate of our evolution toward hybrid 'machines.' I also believe that new and modified materials will become 'smart.' For instance, new materials will be 'self-aware' and will be able to communicate problems in order to avoid failure. Ultimately, these materials will become 'self-healing' and will be able to harness raw materials to manufacture replacement parts in situ. All these materials, and the things built with them will participate in the connected world. We will see continued blurring of the line between 'real' and 'virtual' life." For exaple, artificial general intelligence and quantum computing available in a future version of the cloud connected to individual brain augmentation could make us augmented geniuses, inventing our daily lives in a self-actualization economy as the conscious-technology civilization evolves. Implants in humans that continuously connect them to the web will lead to a loss of privacy and the potential for thought control, decline in autonomy.

● Everyone agrees that the world will be putting AI to work, when internet is improvement to raise robotic efficiency and performance improvement

The technology visionaries surveyed described a much different work environment from the current one. They say remote work arrangements are likely to be the rule, rather than the exception, and virtual assistants will handle many of the mundane and unpleasant tasks currently performed by humans. The shooting is done by a drone guided by a smart guy/gal working a 9-to-5 job in an air-conditioned office in a nice town. Garbage could be picked up, sorted, recycled, all by robots with AI. Tedious surgery completed by robots and teaching via YouTube would leave the humans to the interesting and exciting cases, not the redoing of same lessons to yet more patients/students. Humans could live well on a 20-hour work week with many weeks of paid vacation. Having a job/career could become a positive, not just a necessity. With 24/ 7 learning and just-in-time capacity, people could change areas or careers many times with ease whenever they become bored. This positive outcome is possible if we collectively manage the creation and distribution of the tools and access to the use of new emerging tools. Thus, future everyone will have hundreds of digital workers working for them. Our cognitive mediators will know us in some ways better than we know ourselves. Better episodic memories and large numbers of digital workers will allow expanded entrepreneurship, lifelong learning and focus on transformation.

Thus, our future social development already small world will shrink further as remote collaboration becomes the norm, resulting in major social changes, among them allowing the recent concentration of expertise in major cities to relax and reducing the relevance of national borders. Furthermore, deep learning and AI-assisted technologies for software development and verification, combined with more abstract primitives for executing software in the cloud, will enable even those not trained as software engineers to precisely describe and solve complex problems. I believe the question we're facing is not 'When will machines surpass human intelligence?' but instead 'How can humans work together with machines in new ways?' Rather than worrying about an impending Singularity, I propose the concept of Multiplicity: where diverse combinations of people and machines work together to solve problems and innovate. In analogy with the 1910 High School Movement that was spurred by advances in farm automation, I propose a 'Multiplicity Movement' to evolve the way we learn to emphasize the uniquely human skills that AI and robots cannot replicate: creativity, curiosity, imagination, empathy, human communication, diversity and innovation. AI systems can provide universal access to sophisticated adaptive testing and exercises to discover the unique strengths of each student and to help each student amplify his or her strengths. AI systems could support continuous learning for students of all ages and abilities. Rather than discouraging the human workers of the world with threats of an impending Singularity, let's focus on Multiplicity where advances in AI and robots can inspire us to think deeply about the kind of work we really want to do, how we can change the way we learn and how we might embrace diversity to create myriad new partnerships. So, future AI and internet technoloy will become new partners to assist any business development, even any organizations and social development. Hence, internet improvement must be needed in order to let any businesses can apply robots to raise efficiencies and improve performance more effectively. For example, free internet-connected devices will be available to the poor in exchange for carrying around a sensor that records traffic speed, environmental quality, detailed usage logs, and video and audio recordings (depending on state law). There will be secure vote-by-internet capabilities, through credit card or passport verification, with other secure kiosks available at public facilities (police stations, libraries, fire stations and post offices, should those continue to exist in their current form). Internet and 24/7 real-time connectivity will no longer be viewed as a 'thing' independent from daily life, but integral, like electricity. This has profound psychological implications about what people assume as normal and establishes baseline expectations for access, response times and personalization of functions and information. Contrary to many concerns, as technology becomes more sophisticated, it will ultimately support the primary human drives of social connectedness and agency. As we have seen with social media, first adoption is noncritical – it is a shiny penny for exploration. Then people start making judgments about the value-add based on their own goals and technology companies adapt by designing for more value to the user . Technology is going to change whether we like it or not – expecting it to be worse for individuals means that we look for what's wrong. Expecting it to be better means we look for the strengths and what works and work toward that goal. Technology gives individuals more control – a fundamental human need and a prerequisite to participatory citizenship and collective agency. The danger is that we are so distracted by technology that we forget that digital life is an extension of the offline world and demands the same critical, moral and ethical thinking.

In future 50 years every aspect of our life will be connected, organized and hence, partly controlled, as technology platform and applications businesses will take this opportunity. A few global players will dominate the business; smaller companies (startups) will mostly have a chance in the development sector. Many institutions, such as libraries, will disappear – there might be one or two libraries that function as museums to show how it used to be. People who experienced today's world will definitely value the benefits and amenities they have through technology (human-machine/AI collaboration). If technology becomes part of every aspect of our lives we will have to give up some power and control. People thinking in today's terms will lose a certain amount of freedom, independency and control over their lives. People born after 2030 will probably just think these technologies produced changes that are mostly for the better. It has always been like this – people have always thought/said 'in the old days everything was better. The free, open internet that represented a set of decentralized connections between idiosyncratic actors will be recognized as an aberration in the history of the internet. Today's internet giants will probably be the internet giants of 50 years from now. In recent years, they've made substantial progress in curtailing innovation through acquisitions and copying. As the industry matures, they will add regulatory capture to their skill sets. For many people around the world, the internet will be a set of narrow portals where they exchange their data for a curtailed set of communication, information and consumer services. Thus, digital tools will be part of our body inside and remotely, and will assist us in decision- making constantly, so it will become second nature. Nonetheless, physical feelings will still be exclusively 'physical,' i.e., there will be a significant difference between the 'sensor-based feelings' and real body feelings, so human beings will still have some advantages over technology. This, I believe, will last forever.

CHAPTER THREE

DISCOVERY NEW HEALTH MEDICINE DRUGS

Why do we need to concern new health medicine drugs discovery? I believe that human will face any new kinds of diseases that we had not encountered or contacts in my past. If we lack any new kinds of health medicine drugs discovery to fight any kinds of new diseases in my future. Then, we must face death very easily, such as COVID 19 is one kind of new disease, the another person or other persons can be contacted to cause this kind of COVID 19 disease by the patient's cloths, shoes, hands, even air, mouth of hs body and things. Thus, it had caused many people die in global nowadays. So, medicine or drug or bio-scientists need to spend much time to do any experiment to attempt to discover any new kinds of medicines or drugs to fight any future new kinds of diseases. Otherwise, human will die very easily in soon.

- Why do we need drug discovery?

In the fields of medicine, biotechnology and pharmacology, drug discovery is the process by which new candidate medications are discovered. Historically, drugs were discovered by identifying the active ingredient from traditional remedies or by serendipitous discovery, as with penicillin. More recently, chemical libraries of synthetic small molecules, natural products or extracts were screened in intact cells or whole organisms to identify substances that had a desirable therapeutic effect in a process known as classical pharmacology. After sequencing of the human genome allowed rapid cloning and synthesis of large quantities of purified proteins, it has become common practice to use high throughput screening of large compounds libraries against isolated biological targets which are hypothesized to be disease-modifying in a process known as reverse pharmacology. Hits from these screens are then tested in cells and then in animals for efficacy.

However, modern drug discovery involves the identification of screening hits, medicinal chemistry and optimization of those hits to increase the affinity, selectivity (to reduce the potential of side effects), efficacy/potency, metabolic stability (to increase the half-life), and oral bioavailability. Once a compound that fulfills all of these requirements has been identified, the process of drug development can continue. If successful, clinical trials are developed. Modern drug discovery is thus usually a capital-intensive process that involves large investments by pharmaceutical industry corporations as well as national governments (who provide grants and loan guarantees). Despite advances in technology and understanding of biological systems, drug discovery is still a lengthy, "expensive, difficult, and inefficient process" with low rate of new therapeutic discovery. For example, in 2010, the research and development cost of each new molecular entity was about US$1.8 billion In the 21st century, basic discovery research is funded primarily by governments and by philanthropic organizations, while late-stage development is funded primarily by pharmaceutical companies or venture capitalists. However, discovering drugs that may be a commercial success, or a public health success, involves a complex interaction between investors, industry, academia, patent laws, regulatory exclusivity, marketing and the need to balance secrecy with communication. Meanwhile, for disorders whose rarity means that no large commercial success or public health effect can be expected, the orphan drug funding process ensures that people who experience those disorders can have some hope of pharmacotherapeutic advances.

● Where do new drugs come from? Why does it take so long to get a new drug approved? Why are drugs so expensive?

The medicines we ingest, inject, and inhale are often complex therapeutic compounds. The drugs are usually mixtures of chemicals made from starting materials or drug sources. Depending on the sources from which the drugs were created, the drugs can be categorized as natural, synthetic, or semi-synthetic. Natural drugs are made from compounds found in nature. The most prevalent natural drug sources are plants. The field of science that studies the relationship between people and medicinal plants is known as medicinal ethnobotany. Some examples of medicine that come from plants are morphine (from opium), digoxin (from flower, Digitalis lanata), and aspirin (from willow tree bark). Less prevalent natural drug sources include animals, microbes, and minerals. The first kind drug source is for example, synthetic drugs come from starting materials that are not found in nature. Instead, they are produced by man from smaller chemical building blocks. An example of synthetic medicine is the experimental anti-malaria drug, arterolane. Another kind drug source is semi-synthetic drugs are neither completely natural nor completely synthetic. They are a hybrid. Semi-synthetic drugs are generally made by converting starting materials from natural sources into final products via chemical reactions. Examples of semi-synthetic medicine include the antibiotic, penicillin, and the chemotherapy drug, paclitaxel. To make the chemotherapy drug, paclitaxel, 10-deacetylbaccatin is extracted from yew needles and undergoes a 4-stage synthesis process. They both are the main kinds of drugs manufacturing sources.

● Why does human need new drugs discovery ?

The reason of global health needs demand new approach to drug discovery, the pharmaceutical industry has made enormous strides in the production of potential therapies and medicines. But even today, close to 90% of candidate drugs that enter Phase 1 trials fail to make it to the market place. This is a system beset by duplication of effort and hence wastage of resources. No one lab or institution can do this on its own. We must urgently pool resources and expertise, minimise duplication, explore new drug targets, biomarkers, and technologies in order to generate new, effective, and more affordable drugs for patients more quickly.

Discovey of any one kind of new drug, it needs long time to experiment. It must come up with new ways to accelerate our drug discovery process. Alternatively, we must entirely rethink how we treat illness. This is not just limited to bacterial infections. We need to invent better ways to combat all forms of disease. The process of discovering, testing, and approving a drug for commercial use can take 20 years and over of 1 billion dollars. Obviously, decreasing both the time and the cost of developing these drugs can save many lives. There are some new technologies which are already helping to ramp up this process. For example, computational modeling of drugs has massively sped up the screening process for drugs. We can now take thousands of potential drug candidates and narrow them down to a couple viable options. But there are more ways we can expedite this process.

A recent estimate states that we now know the molecular cause of over 4,000 diseases — but we only have drugs for about 250. How can we do better? The FDA approval process is long and arduous. Even for compounds that have been approved in other countries, FDA trials can be drawn out for years. The FDA approval process can be responsible for about 25% of the cost of a drug and can delay the arrival of a drug over 10 years. There is even data that suggests that the FDA kills many more by not approving drugs than it ever saves by approving drugs (for more on the harmful effects of the FDA, see Cato, Forbes, The Independent Institute, and LifeExtension). By delaying good drugs that can save lives, and by doing little to stop bad drugs, the FDA is often an inhibitor to the medical process. We need to rethink the FDA if we want to streamline the drug discovery process. If we can change many FDA policies, we will see more drugs created for those 4,000 known targets.

● The process of new drug experiment success time evaluation

Any new kind of drugs experiment success, they must experience these processes. They may include:

1 Drug testing and licensing

All new drugs and treatments have to be thoroughly tested before they are licensed and available for patients. A new drug is first studied in the laboratory. If it looks promising, it is carefully studied in people. If trials show that it works well and doesn't cause too many side effects, it may be licensed. You may hear this process called 'from bench to bedside. There is no typical length of time it takes for a drug to be tested and approved. It might take 10 to 15 years or more to complete all 3 phases of clinical trials before the licensing stage. But this time span varies a lot. There are many factors that affect how long it takes for a drug to be licensed.

2 Factors that affect how long trials take

The type of cancer drug success experiement needs time

Clinical trials for rarer cancers often take longer because there are fewer patients available to take part. Research teams from several different countries may need to collaborate so there are enough patients. This can mean the trial takes longer to organise and set up. But international trials can often recruit people more quickly and so are likely be quicker in the long run.
Researchers running clinical trials for more common cancers are generally able to find enough people to take part more easily.

3 The type of treatment

Trials that use new methods of giving treatment, such as a new way to give radiotherapy for example, may take longer to set up and run. This is because the research teams need specialist equipment and extra training. These trials may only be able to run in a small number of hospitals compared to trials using standard ways of giving treatment. How long treatment takes can also affect the results. It is likely to be quicker to get results for a trial looking at a single dose or short course of treatment, compared to a treatment that lasts for months or even years.

4 The type of trial

Some trials look at treatments to prevent cancer or ways of screening for cancer. Screening means testing for cancer in people who don't have any signs or symptoms. People who join these trials haven't been diagnosed with cancer. The research team will often want to follow them for many years to see who develops cancer and who doesn't. They will then compare the different trial groups to see if a particular treatment can help prevent cancer or whether a test can help to diagnose it early.These trials often take a long time to get results compared to treatment trials. It can take years to see a clear difference in the number of people in the different groups who go on to develop cancer. So, any new kinds of drug research experiements, they depend on the number of patients needed in order to decide whether how drug quality level, how many drugs manufacturing supply number, drug price in global market.

Statistics experts look at what the research team want to find out and the design of the trial, and then work out how many patients are needed. If there aren't enough patients taking part, the results may not be reliable. The number of people they need to get reliable results will depend on how many treatment groups there are and exactly what the research team want to find out.

5 The follow up period

Research teams look at how well people are doing for some time after they have treatment as part of a trial. This is to see how well the treatment works over a longer period of time, and to find out more about long term side effects. Follow up periods can range from a few months to more than 10 years, depending on the type of treatment and the group of patients. Or maybe longer for a trial looking at screening or prevention.

6 Any problems with the new treatment

There may be problems with new drugs or treatments that the researchers don't know about until they run the trials. There could be unexpected side effects or reactions to treatment. Or there may be difficulties in giving the treatment to patients. Problems with the new treatment may mean the trial takes longer to complete.

Thus, any kinds of new drug experiement need long time to be attempted to carry on, every new kind of drug experiment is evaluated about 10 to 20 , even more time. So, future drug scientists have responsibilities to evaluate whether which kinds of diseases will cause in order to concentrate on spending time to carry on researching the kind of new drug experiment. It aims to use limited resource and time to let patients to get health.

CHAPTER FOUR

IMPROVING LIVING ENVIRONMENT

What are the disadvantages if we do not concern how to improve our global living environment? I shall explain as below:

- reasons to improve living environment

Nowadays, as population on the earth keeps expanding, human needs increase endlessly causing more global environmental problems to proliferate globally. Global environmental crisis has become an unequivocal fact that can affect our livelihood and it is capable of changing the current landscape drastically. Hence, people hold the responsibility to tackle current global environmental issues to make this world a better place. With destructive natural disasters like flash floods or snowstorm as well as the changing of weather patterns, the earth is poised at the precarious verge of severe environmental crisis. Human intervention has caused many dysfunctions to the environment, some of which have left damages on the ecosystem that eliminates other sources of necessity to other living things. Ever since humans start to harvest the Earth 's resources, many landscapes have been altered to fit the lifestyles of countless inhabitants. So people ought to be aware of other types of environmental challenges that the planet is facing. Some of the challenges that the planet is facing include overpopulation of human beings that leads to natural resources depletion, deforestation and loss of biodiversity, acid rain and ocean acidification, pollution and waste disposal. Thus, it seems that global living environment and pollution have close relationship. I mean that air and water and paste and chemical pollution will reduce if we can keep our global living environment more clean, safe and without more rubblishs are allowed to keep in our living places, even gardens, public places anywhere.

One of the key ethical questions is whether a life-extension pill would extend our healthy years or simply prolong frailty towards the end of life. Better health and longer life would certainly be an attractive prospect for many people. If we were healthier for longer then perhaps we could achieve more of our ambitions and engage in the things we enjoy for longer. But some people worry that our lives may be extended in a state of low quality of life rather than health. Although this is not the goal, critics worry that it might be an unintended consequence of intervention in ageing and longevity. As with all pharmaceuticals, both health benefits and risks need to be considered. If life span could be extended a great deal – perhaps to more than 100 years or even longer – then some other interesting issues might arise. For instance, would we simply run out of things to do and become bored? Even things that we enjoy may become stale after several centuries. How long would we have to work for? If our lives were 200 years long then it is unlikely that many people could afford to retire at 65. However, this may also present new opportunities such as having several different careers within a lifetime. If our future earth can not provide a health and clean living environment to let human to live, then our quality of living must be worse to compare nowadays, it will cause our next generation can not be health to live ot they will have many different kinds of disease, such as COV19 disease , or future there are many kinds of serious disease to compare COV19 disease , they will bring threats to influence our next generation to live in anywhere health places in our earth. It is very disappointment to us, such as our next generation's parents, we have not feel responsibilities to keep our living environment to be improved to let our next generation to live in global anywhere clean and health living environment. So, we need to concern how to improve our living environment nowadays.

However, I shall suggest these methods how to improve our living environment to be better. If we can be habit to do environment protection behaviors every day, then our living environment must be influenced to improve more easily and rapidly, in society, individual sand businessmen and our governments have resposibilities, they may include as below:

- Individual and businessmen and governments how to improve living environment

Individual responsibilities to improving living environment

1. Use Reusable Bags

Plastic grocery-type bags that get thrown out end up in landfills or in other parts of the environment. These can suffocate animals who get stuck in them or may mistake them for food. Also, it takes a while for the bags to decompose. Whether you are shopping for food, clothes or books, use a reusable bag. This cuts down on litter and prevents animals from getting a hold of them. There are even some stores (such as Target) that offer discounts for using reusable bags! These bags are useful for things other than shopping as well. I have heard of people using reusable bags when they move! If you forget your bags at home, buy a new one. Better yet, keep a couple bags in your car so you never leave home without them (just make sure you remember you put them there)! If you are in a position where you need to use the plastic bags, reuse them the next time you go shopping, or use them for something else. Just do not be so quick to throw them out!

There are some states that are outlawing or charging extra for using plastic bags. Using reusable bags helps the environment AND your budget!

2. Print as Little as Necessary

We have all had that teacher that wanted us to have a copy of every single reading when we come to class, or that professor who wanted a hard copy of the ten-page paper that is due next week. These are fine but it seems as if they do not understand that using so much paper is detrimental to the environment. What can you do? Ask your teacher if you can bring a laptop or an e-reader to class so that you can download the reading onto that and read it from there. If not, print on both sides of the page to reduce the amount of paper used. If you need to turn in a long paper, ask the professor if it is okay to print on both sides of the page and explain why you're asking. Most teachers care about the environment as well and would be willing to allow you to do so.

3. Recycle

Recycling is such a simple thing to do, but so many people don't do it. Many garbage disposal companies offer recycling services, so check with the company you use to see if they can help you get started! It is as simple as getting a bin and putting it out with your trash cans for free! Another way to recycle is to look for recycling cans near trashcans. Instead of throwing recyclables in the trash with your non-recyclables, make a point to take an extra step to locate recycling cans around your campus.

4. Use a Reusable Beverage Containers

Instead of buying individually-packaged drinks, consider buying a bulk container of the beverage you want and buying a reusable water bottle. Not only will this help the environment, but it will also help you save money since you are buying a bulk container. Many campuses offer water fountains designed for drinking as well as for refilling reusable water bottles. Make use of these fountains throughout the day when you finish off the initial beverage.

Along these lines, many restaurants offer reusable containers for drinks. If you go to a certain place a lot, consider buying one of these containers to help minimize waste. A lot of coffee shops even offer a discount to customers who use a reusable container for their drinks. Starbucks, as an example, offers a small discount for customers who do this. Saving the environment and money?

5. Save Water

Water is wasted more frequently than we can see. Turn off the faucet as you are brushing your teeth. Don't turn your shower on until you're ready to get in and wash your hair. Limit your water usage as you wash dishes. Changing old habits will be good for both the environment and your wallet!

6. Avoid Taking Cars or Carpool When Possible

Cars are harmful to the environment. Taking public transportation, walking, or riding a bike to class are better options that help the environment and your budget, as well as getting some exercise in! If you do need to use your car, compare schedules and places of residency with those in your classes. You can split the cost of gas and have alternating schedules for who drives when. This is cheaper than everyone driving separately and you'll be closer with friends!

Businessmen responsibilities to improving living environment

Instead of individuals have respobsibilities to improve our living environment. Businessmen have also responsibilities to improve our living environment. I shall indicate mining businessmen example to explain how mining businesses may influence our living environment to be worse. The disadvantages of mining include harm to air pollution, water pollution, loss of usable land, destruction of animal habitat, and harm to local communities and the miners themselves. While mining produces the resources needed for fuel, electronics, and other items as well as jobs, companies often don't factor the harm mining can do into their decision making. Below factors may influence our global living environment to be worse as below:

Air Pollution

Lead, arsenic, cadmium, and other harmful substance As are often exposed by mining and picked up by the wind, causing allergies and breathing problems in local people. Mining machinery uses fossil fuels and releases large amounts of carbon dioxide and other substances that contribute to global warming.

Water Pollution

Mining can cause metal contamination and acid mine drainage that makes water unsafe for plants and animals. Sediments released by mining choke streams and erode soil. Both of these problems also cause problems for farming and the water people drink.

Loss of Usable Land

Mining, especially open pit mining, destroys land that can be used for farming, houses, and other human purposes, often permanently. Entire mountains and rivers can be destroyed. Loss of soil and deep underground excavation can also make land unstable and collapse.

Destruction of Animal Habitats

Mining also has disadvantages for plants and wildlife. It destroys homes and food sources for animals and leads to less diverse plant and animal life. Endangered species that are already sensitive to changes in their environment are especially at risk. Because mining releases toxins that linger for years later, the damage to plants and animals often isn't fully understood until after mining has ended.

Harm to Miners

Mining is dangerous for the people who do it, especially for miners who work underground. Breathing in mineral dust can cause deadly diseases like pneumoconiosis or black lung, while the machinery used often causes hearing loss. Back injuries and other physical problems are also common in miners. While big disasters often show up in the news, many of the miners who are killed or injured on the job never receive media attention. In 2010, almost 2,500 miners died from causes other than major accidents.

Consequences for Local Communities

Mining is also harmful to the communities that support mines. Mining can lead to loss of homes, land, and clean water, and it often releases chemicals into the environment that cause health problems for locals. Mines also need large amounts of water to operate, which leaves less for people to drink or farm with. It also causes less obvious problems. Because only some people in an area benefit from mining, but everyone faces at least some of the disadvantages, mining can divide communities. It can also lead to harassment or abuse from corporate or government officials who care more about the profits of mining than the people it affects. The secrecy around mining and who makes money from it often makes this disadvantage even worse.

Thus, ourselves and businessmen can not neglect our any activities can influence global living environment to be worse. We need to learn how to avoid to do any bad behaviors to influence our future global living environment to be worse, even the worst.

Governments responsibilities to improving living environment

Any country's government needs to concern social responsibility before it decides to implement any sustainable development. Because although sustainable development may bring some benefits to some countries, but it can also bring disadvantages to themselves countries. What Are Disadvantages of Sustainable Development? It may brins these disadvantages as below:

Increased Costs

Because sustainable development relies on newer technologies and materials that cost more to produce, the overall costs are often more than that of traditional construction. The higher cost of materials is passed on to developers. Developers pass it on to property owners, who pass it on to tenants. Future development will include tools that haven't even been invented yet. The trial and error of using new materials and ideas can also bring costs up for everyone.

Lower Quality of Life for Some Elements of Society

Sustainable development will shrink or do away with certain job sectors. This will lead to job loss for some workers. The fossil fuel industry could see plants close and employees lose jobs as sustainable development relies on new energy sources. The rising costs and less robust power of alternative energy can also lead to a lower quality of life for people who live in sustainably developed areas.

Resistance to New Methods

When people try to implement new ideas, there's naturally a certain amount of resistance. People in general are set in their ways and don't want to change their lives radically. As more governments and companies attempt to put sustainable development into practice, more resistance will follow.

Some of the resistance will come in the form of people who initially adopt the idea of sustainable development with enthusiasm, but their commitment shrinks as they start to put new ideas into practice. Contractors and tenants may resist a specific initiative because it forces them to change the ways they work and live.

Increased Regulation

Sustainable approaches will naturally lead to increased regulation on construction and the daily operation of businesses. A greater commitment to the environment will lead to tighter controls on how people live their lives. Stricter building codes and tougher emission standards are likely. While some people will accept a greater burden of regulation because they see the overall benefit, many people will disagree with government intruding into their lives.

Political Struggle

In addition to the public resistance, there's a political cost to committing to the environment. The deep political divides in society mean that some political powers won't want to commit to sustainable initiatives. Certain industries will try to influence politicians via lobbyists. Some politicians will be completely against sustainable development.

Is It Worth the Trouble?

People and organizations that are in favor of sustainable development believe that it's worth moving past these disadvantages to work on the environment. Advocates say that sustainable development is an investment in future generations. The biggest defenders of these initiatives are working on ways of overcoming the hurdles.

Thus, ineffective or poor sustainable development may also bring poor living environment, due to wrong sustainable development to the country. For example, if Afria government only concern how to find mining lands for sustinable development, but it neglects to keep clean and health and natural land living environment to African to continue to live. Then, it will reduce African quality of living to be worse. So, any countries governments need to keep balance to bring social benefit when they decide to do sustainable development in themselves countries.

Printed by Libri Plureos GmbH in Hamburg,
Germany